A Grateful Heart

Importance of Sharing Testimonies of GOD's Grace

Gerard Assey

A Grateful Heart:
Importance of Sharing Testimonies of GOD's Grace

By

Gerard Assey

Published by:
Gerard Assey
19/18, Palli Arasan Street
Anna Nagar East
Chennai - 600 102

ISBN: 978-81-967202-9-2

Image courtesy Freepik: https://www.freepik.com

Table of Contents

Introduction

In a world filled with the noise and chaos of modern life, it's easy to lose sight of one of the most profound and transformative emotions that can enrich our souls - gratitude. Gratitude is not just a simple thank you; it is a powerful force that can shape our lives, our relationships, and our connection with the divine. In this chapter, we will delve into the concept of gratitude and its significance in our spiritual and personal growth. We will explore how this age-old virtue can lead to a more fulfilling, joyful, and meaningful existence, and we will do so through the lens of biblical inspiration, exemplified by Jesus' encouragement in Luke 8.39 to share one's testimony of God's work.

Gratitude, at its core, is the act of acknowledging the goodness in our lives and expressing appreciation for it. It is the recognition of the blessings, both big and small, that we receive daily. Gratitude is a stance of the heart, an attitude, and a way of life that enables us to find joy and contentment even in the most challenging circumstances. This chapter will explore the extraordinary power that gratitude holds, not only in our own personal lives but also in our relationships with others and, most importantly, our relationship with the divine.

Gratitude and Spiritual Growth

Spiritual growth is often characterized by an ever-deepening awareness of the divine and a closer alignment with our core values. Gratitude plays a significant role in this process. As we express gratitude for the blessings we've received, we become more attuned to the presence of God in our lives. Gratitude becomes a form of worship, a way to honor and connect with the divine source of all goodness.

In the Bible, the act of gratitude is woven throughout the Old and New Testaments. Countless verses and stories remind us of the importance of being thankful. One of the most striking examples is found in Luke 8.39, where Jesus heals a man possessed by demons and instructs him, "Return to your home, and declare how much God has done for you." This command encapsulates the essence of gratitude and the power it holds. It's not just about feeling thankful in your heart; it's about sharing the testimony of God's work in your life with others.

Gratitude and Personal Growth

Gratitude is not limited to its impact on our spiritual journey. It extends its influence into our personal growth and overall well-being. When we practice gratitude, we shift our focus from what we lack to what we have. This shift in perspective can lead to increased happiness, reduced stress, improved mental health, and stronger relationships. Gratitude allows us to savor the present moment, fostering mindfulness and a sense of inner peace.

Moreover, gratitude is not solely a reaction to positive experiences. It is a choice, a conscious decision to find the silver lining in even the most challenging situations. As we cultivate gratitude, we become more resilient and better equipped to handle life's ups and downs. Our character is refined, and our capacity for empathy and compassion expands.

In the pages that follow, we will explore how gratitude can transform your life in countless ways. We will delve into the psychological and spiritual benefits of practicing gratitude, share personal anecdotes that illustrate its profound impact, and provide practical guidance on how to cultivate this virtue in your daily life.

As we embark on this journey to understand the power of gratitude, remember the words of Jesus in Luke 8.39. Just as the healed man was instructed to declare "how much God has done for you," we, too, are called to share the abundance of blessings in our lives and encourage others to embrace gratitude as a path to spiritual and personal growth.

The Power of Gratitude

Gratitude is a transformative force that has the potential to reshape our lives in profound ways. It is a concept that reaches across time and cultures, transcending the boundaries of faith and spirituality. In this chapter, we will delve deep into the transformative power of gratitude, exploring its psychological and spiritual benefits, and we'll support our understanding with relevant Bible verses, detailed explanations, stories from both the Old and New Testaments, and actionable plans to incorporate gratitude into your daily life.

Transformative Power of Gratitude

Gratitude is not merely a fleeting emotion or a polite expression of thanks; it is a powerful perspective that can reframe our lives. When we embrace gratitude, we shift our focus from what we lack to what we have. This simple shift in perspective can lead to a cascade of positive changes.

Psychological Benefits of Gratitude

The psychological benefits of gratitude are extensive and well-documented. It has been linked to increased happiness, reduced stress and depression, improved sleep, and enhanced overall well-being. When we consciously practice gratitude, we train our minds to focus on the positive aspects of life, even in the face of adversity.

One relevant biblical verse that highlights the psychological benefits of gratitude is Philippians 4:6-7: "Do not be anxious about anything, but in every situation, by prayer and petition, with thanksgiving, present your requests to God. And the peace of God, which transcends all understanding, will guard your hearts and your minds in Christ Jesus." This verse emphasizes that through thanksgiving and gratitude, we can find peace and solace, even in times of turmoil.

Spiritual Benefits of Gratitude

From a spiritual perspective, gratitude is a form of worship. It is an expression of acknowledgment for the blessings we receive from a higher power. Gratitude deepens our connection with the divine, making us more attuned to the presence of God in our lives.

A relevant biblical verse is Psalm 100:4-5: "Enter his gates with thanksgiving and his courts with praise; give thanks to him and praise his name. For the Lord is good and his love endures forever; his faithfulness continues through all generations." This passage underscores the idea that gratitude is an integral part of worship and recognizing God's goodness.

Stories from the Old Testament

The Old Testament is replete with stories that exemplify the power of gratitude. For instance, the story of Job, a man who faced unimaginable trials and tribulations yet maintained his gratitude and faith in God. Despite losing his wealth, health, and family, he proclaimed, "Naked I came from my mother's womb, and naked shall I return there; the Lord gave, and the Lord has taken away; blessed be the name of the Lord" (Job 1:21). Job's unwavering gratitude in the face of suffering teaches us that gratitude can sustain us through life's harshest challenges.

Stories from the New Testament

In the New Testament, we see Jesus Himself as the embodiment of gratitude. The miracle of the feeding of the five thousand is a prime example. In Matthew 14:19, Jesus "took the five loaves and the two fish, and looking up to heaven, he gave thanks and broke the loaves." Here, Jesus sets a powerful example of offering gratitude to God even in the face of scarcity. This act of thanksgiving resulted in an abundance that fed thousands.

Action Plans for Practicing Gratitude

- ✓ **Daily Gratitude Journal**: Start a journal where you record three things you are grateful for each day. This simple practice can help you maintain a grateful perspective.
- ✓ **Mindful Thankfulness**: Throughout your day, pause to consciously acknowledge the blessings in your life. This mindfulness practice can help you stay attuned to gratitude.
- ✓ **Express Your Gratitude**: Make it a habit to express your gratitude to others. A simple thank you can make a world of difference in someone's day.
- ✓ **Prayer of Thanks**: In your daily prayers, incorporate a specific time to express your gratitude to God for the blessings you've received.
- ✓ **Acts of Service**: Engage in acts of kindness and service to others. This not only fosters gratitude within you but also spreads it to those you help.

Journaling Prompts:

- ✓ What are three things you are grateful for today, and why?
- ✓ How has practicing gratitude made a difference in your life?
- ✓ Reflect on a challenging situation you faced. How did gratitude help you navigate it?

Reflection Exercises:

- ✓ Keep a gratitude journal for a week, noting at least one thing you're thankful for each day.
- ✓ Share your gratitude journey with a friend or family member and discuss the impact it has had on your life.
- ✓ Practice a gratitude meditation where you focus on the things you're thankful for and let go of negativity.

Action Plan

Instructions: Use this worksheet to create a personalized action plan based on the insights gained from this chapter. Reflect on your own experiences and set concrete goals for cultivating gratitude.

Gratitude Journal:

- ☐ Commit to starting a gratitude journal.
- ☐ Set a specific time each day for journaling.
- ☐ List three things you're grateful for today.

Sharing Gratitude:

- ☐ Choose a close friend or family member to share your moments of gratitude.
- ☐ Plan a conversation to express your appreciation for each other.

Gratitude Meditation:

- ☐ Explore meditation resources or apps for gratitude.

- Schedule regular sessions for gratitude meditation.

Impact of Gratitude:

- Reflect on a challenging situation where gratitude could have made a difference.
- Set a goal to apply gratitude in a challenging scenario.

As you embark deeper on your journey of gratitude, remember that it is not just an emotion; it is a way of life. Through gratitude, you can experience profound transformation, both psychologically and spiritually, and align your heart with the divine purpose. In the chapters that follow, we will continue to explore how gratitude can enrich your life and inspire you to share your testimony of God's work in your life.

Why Share Testimonies?

Sharing testimonies is a practice deeply rooted in gratitude and faith. In this chapter, we will explore the profound significance of sharing testimonies as an act of gratitude and how these narratives can inspire and uplift not only the storyteller but also others who hear them. We'll delve into the biblical precedent for sharing testimonies, providing relevant verses, detailed explanations, and examples from both the Old and New Testaments. Additionally, we will offer actionable plans for incorporating testimony-sharing into your spiritual journey.

Significance of Sharing Testimonies as an Act of Gratitude

Sharing testimonies is an act of gratitude because it involves acknowledging and declaring the goodness and grace of God in our lives. When we recount the ways in which God has worked in our favor, we are not only expressing our thankfulness, but we are also providing a powerful testament to God's faithfulness and love.

In Psalm 107:2-3, we find this expression of gratitude: "Let the redeemed of the Lord tell their story—those he redeemed from the hand of the foe, those he gathered from the lands, from east and west, from north and south." This verse exemplifies the importance of sharing the story of redemption, highlighting the role of gratitude in giving testimony.

Testimonies also serve as a reminder of God's faithfulness, both to the storyteller and to those who hear the story. They provide a tangible record of

God's work, which can be revisited in times of doubt or hardship.

How Testimonies Inspire and Uplift Others

Testimonies are not just personal anecdotes; they are sources of inspiration and hope. When we share our stories of how God has intervened in our lives, we offer others a glimpse into the boundless love and power of the divine. Such narratives can be especially comforting during moments of struggle and uncertainty.

In 2 Corinthians 1:3-4, the Apostle Paul wrote, "Praise be to the God and Father of our Lord Jesus Christ, the Father of compassion and the God of all comfort, who comforts us in all our troubles so that we can comfort those in any trouble with the comfort we ourselves receive from God." This passage emphasizes that our testimonies of God's comfort can be a source of solace and encouragement for others facing similar trials.

Sharing testimonies not only uplifts others but also fosters a sense of unity and community. It connects individuals on a deeper level as they witness the shared experiences of faith and grace.

Biblical Precedent for Sharing Testimonies

Throughout the Bible, we find numerous instances where people shared their testimonies. In the Old Testament, we see the Israelites commemorating their deliverance from Egypt through the celebration of Passover. This annual event involved the retelling of their testimony, reminding them of God's mighty acts.

In the New Testament, we see Paul sharing his testimony multiple times, recounting his conversion on the road to Damascus and how he came to follow Christ. These testimonies were not only personal but also powerful tools for spreading the message of Christianity.

Action Plans for Sharing Testimonies

- ✓ **Reflection and Writing**: Begin by reflecting on significant moments in your life when you experienced God's grace. Write down your testimony, making it personal and relatable.
- ✓ **Share in a Safe Space**: Start by sharing your testimony with a trusted friend or within your church or faith community. This can help you gain confidence in sharing your story.
- ✓ **Practice Active Listening**: Be attentive when others share their testimonies. Offer support and encouragement, as you would hope to receive when sharing your own.
- ✓ **Use Technology**: In today's digital age, consider using technology to share your testimony. You can write a blog, record a podcast, or create a video to reach a wider audience.
- ✓ **Pray for Opportunities**: Pray for opportunities to share your testimony, and ask for guidance to discern when and with whom to share.

Journaling Prompts:

- ✓ Have you ever shared a personal testimony of God's work in your life? If so, how did it feel? If not, what has held you back?
- ✓ Reflect on a time when someone else's testimony inspired you. What impact did it have on your faith or outlook?

- ✓ What do you think are the most compelling reasons to share your testimony with others?

Reflection Exercises:

- ✓ Write down the key moments in your life where you've experienced God's grace and intervention.
- ✓ Discuss with a group the significance of sharing testimonies and how it can inspire faith and unity.
- ✓ Make a commitment to share your testimony with at least one person in the coming month.

Action Plan

Instructions: Use this worksheet to create an action plan for sharing your own testimonies and appreciating the significance of sharing testimonies with others.

Personal Testimony:

- ☐ Identify a personal experience where you've encountered God's grace.
- ☐ Craft a brief outline of your testimony, highlighting key moments.

Significance of Sharing:

- ☐ Reflect on the impact of sharing testimonies in building faith and community.
- ☐ List three key takeaways from the chapter about sharing testimonies.

Listening and Learning:

- ☐ Seek out platforms or events where you can listen to others' testimonies.
- ☐ Take notes on testimonies that inspire you and consider their impact.

Sharing Your Own Testimony:

- ☐ Choose a trusted friend or mentor to share your testimony with.

- Set a date for sharing your testimony and prepare your message.

In conclusion, sharing testimonies is a profound act of gratitude, inspiring and uplifting both the storyteller and those who listen. By exploring the biblical precedent for testimony-sharing and incorporating these practices into your spiritual journey, you can deepen your faith and contribute to a sense of community and hope among fellow believers. In the following chapters, we will continue to explore the role of gratitude and testimony in personal and spiritual growth.

Building a Grateful Heart

A grateful heart is not something we are born with; it is a quality we can nurture and cultivate. In this chapter, we will explore practical advice and exercises to help you develop a grateful heart. We will delve into the role of prayer, meditation, and mindfulness in this process, as well as provide personal stories that showcase how individuals have transformed their lives through gratitude. Throughout, we will refer to relevant Bible verses, offer explanations, share details, and provide examples from both the Old and New Testaments. Additionally, we will provide actionable plans for readers to practice gratitude.

Practical Advice for Cultivating a Grateful Heart

- ✓ **Gratitude Journal**: Start a daily or weekly gratitude journal. Each day, list things you're thankful for. This exercise helps shift your focus towards the positive.
- ✓ **Acts of Kindness**: Engage in acts of kindness towards others. Helping others can generate feelings of gratitude and fulfillment.
- ✓ **Positive Affirmations**: Use positive affirmations to remind yourself of the things you're grateful for. Affirmations can reinforce a positive mindset.
- ✓ **Surround Yourself with Positivity**: Spend time with people who radiate positivity and gratitude. Their energy can be contagious.
- ✓ **Limit Negative Influences**: Minimize exposure to negative news, social media, or

other sources that can bring you down. Focus on uplifting content instead.

The Role of Prayer, Meditation, and Mindfulness

Prayer: Prayer is a powerful tool for cultivating gratitude. Through prayer, you can express your thankfulness to God, seek guidance, and reflect on the blessings in your life. Philippians 4:6 encourages us to, "Do not be anxious about anything, but in every situation, by prayer and petition, with thanksgiving, present your requests to God."

Meditation: Meditation allows you to be still, reflect, and center your thoughts. Mindful meditation can help you become aware of the present moment and the gifts it holds. Meditate on verses like Psalm 34:1, "I will bless the Lord at all times; his praise shall continually be in my mouth."

Mindfulness: Being mindful involves paying attention to the details of life, both big and small. Mindfulness practice enables you to recognize the beauty and blessings that often go unnoticed in the rush of daily living.

Personal Stories of Transformation through Gratitude

Throughout history, countless individuals have experienced transformation through the practice of gratitude. One such example comes from the life of Corrie ten Boom, a Christian who, along with her family, helped Jews escape the Nazis during World War II. After being imprisoned in a concentration camp, she emerged with a heart filled with gratitude. She once said, "I discovered that when I am thankful, the darkness leaves."

Examples from the Old Testament

In the Old Testament, we find the story of Hannah in 1 Samuel 1:1-20. Hannah's deep desire for a child led her to pray earnestly. When her prayer was answered, she expressed her gratitude with a heartfelt song of praise. This story exemplifies how gratitude can emerge from the depths of one's heart when prayers are answered.

Examples from the New Testament

In the New Testament, we see the story of the ten lepers in Luke 17:11-19. When Jesus healed them, only one, a Samaritan, returned to give thanks. This account highlights the power of gratitude to change lives and its importance in our relationship with God.

Action Plans for Cultivating Gratitude

- ✓ **Morning Gratitude Ritual**: Begin each day by naming three things you're grateful for. Make this a daily practice.
- ✓ **Gratitude Walk**: Go for a walk, focusing on the beauty of nature around you. Reflect on the things you're grateful for during the walk.
- ✓ **Serve Others**: Volunteer or engage in acts of service. Helping others can deepen your appreciation for what you have.
- ✓ **Gratitude Letters**: Write letters of gratitude to people who have impacted your life positively.
- ✓ **Gratitude Challenges**: Participate in gratitude challenges on social media or with friends to stay committed to a grateful mindset.

Journaling Prompts:

- ✓ What are some practical ways you can incorporate gratitude into your daily life?

- ✓ How has prayer or meditation helped you cultivate a grateful heart?
- ✓ Reflect on a time when you witnessed someone else's gratitude transform their life. What did you learn from their experience?

Reflection Exercises:

- ✓ Create a gratitude jar where you write down things you're thankful for and add them daily. Review the notes at the end of the month.
- ✓ Practice a mindfulness exercise where you focus on the present moment and list the things you appreciate in that moment.
- ✓ Challenge yourself to replace negative thoughts with thoughts of gratitude for a day.

Action Plan

Instructions: Use this worksheet to create a personalized action plan for building a grateful heart. Set practical goals and explore ways to cultivate gratitude in your daily life.

Mindfulness and Awareness:

- ☐ Integrate mindfulness into your daily life by practicing present-moment awareness.
- ☐ Identify specific times during the day to be mindful of blessings.

Acts of Kindness and Generosity:

- ☐ Plan acts of kindness or generosity toward others.
- ☐ Record your experiences and their impact on your gratitude.

Gratitude Journal:

- ☐ Commit to maintaining a gratitude journal.
- ☐ Specify the frequency and length of journaling sessions.

Replacing Negativity:

- Pay attention to negative thoughts and reactions.
- Set a goal to replace negative thoughts with gratitude in specific situations.

In conclusion, building a grateful heart is a transformative process that can bring joy and contentment to your life. Through practical exercises, mindfulness, and inspiration from personal stories and biblical examples, you can nurture this virtue. As you incorporate these practices into your daily routine, you will find that gratitude becomes a natural and enduring part of your life. In the chapters that follow, we will continue to explore the power of gratitude and how it can inspire you to share your testimony.

Importance of Testimonies

In this chapter, we will explore the profound significance of testimonies in the context of the Bible. We will delve deeper into the biblical examples of testimonies, both in the Old and New Testaments, to showcase how individuals shared their experiences and encounters with God. We will also discuss the enduring impact of these testimonies on faith and community, providing relevant Bible verses, detailed explanations, examples from both testaments, and actionable plans for readers to put into practice.

Biblical Examples of Testimonies

In the Bible, testimonies are not just narratives; they are powerful tools for conveying the faithfulness and goodness of God. They serve as a way to record and pass down God's actions and interventions in the lives of individuals and the community. Here are some examples from both the Old and New Testaments:

Old Testament Examples

- ✓ **The Exodus**: The Israelites' liberation from slavery in Egypt is a central testimony in the Old Testament. The Passover celebration, which commemorates this event, involves recounting the story of their deliverance. The act of sharing this testimony was a way to remember God's faithfulness and a commandment to pass it down through generations.
- ✓ **Joshua's Covenant**: In Joshua 24, Joshua gathers the Israelites and recounts God's faithfulness throughout their history. He

challenges them to choose whom they will serve but declares, "As for me and my household, we will serve the Lord" (Joshua 24:15). This serves as a powerful personal testimony within the broader context of the community's faith.

New Testament Examples

- ✓ **The Woman at the Well**: In John 4:1-42, we find the story of the Samaritan woman who met Jesus at the well. After her encounter with Jesus, she went back to her village to testify about Him, leading many to believe in Him. Her testimony had a profound impact on her community.
- ✓ **The Apostles' Testimonies**: In the book of Acts, we see the early disciples and apostles sharing their personal testimonies of encountering the resurrected Christ and the transformation it brought to their lives. These testimonies played a vital role in the spread of Christianity.

Enduring Impact of Testimonies

Testimonies in the Bible have had an enduring impact on faith and community. They serve several crucial purposes:

- ✓ **Strengthening Faith**: Testimonies serve to strengthen the faith of those who share them and those who hear them. They provide evidence of God's existence, love, and faithfulness.
- ✓ **Passing Down Faith**: Testimonies are a way of passing down faith from one generation to the next. They serve as a living history of God's actions among His people.

- ✓ **Inspiring Witness**: Testimonies inspire others to witness God's work in their own lives. They encourage individuals to seek a personal relationship with God.
- ✓ **Fostering Community**: Testimonies create a sense of community as people share their faith journeys. They build connections among believers, reinforcing the idea that they are not alone in their faith.

Action Plans for Sharing Testimonies

- ✓ **Start with a Personal Testimony**: Begin by crafting your own personal testimony. Reflect on how God has worked in your life, the challenges you've faced, and how your faith has grown.
- ✓ **Share within Your Faith Community**: Share your testimony within your church or faith community. This is a supportive environment where you can practice sharing your story.
- ✓ **Use Technology**: In the digital age, consider creating a blog, podcast, or video to share your testimony with a wider audience.
- ✓ **Be Authentic**: When sharing your testimony, be authentic and vulnerable. People connect with real, relatable stories.
- ✓ **Listen to Others**: Be an active listener when others share their testimonies. Encourage them and offer support.

Journaling Prompts:

- ✓ List three biblical examples of testimonies that have inspired you and explain why.

- ✓ How do you think sharing testimonies strengthens faith and builds a sense of community?
- ✓ Reflect on a time when you heard a personal testimony that had a lasting impact on your beliefs or actions.

Reflection Exercises:

- ✓ Gather with a group and share your favorite biblical testimonies. Discuss what you find most inspiring in each story.
- ✓ Attend a testimony-sharing event or church service and reflect on how the testimonies affected your own faith.
- ✓ Write down your own personal testimony and identify key lessons or themes that others can draw from it.

Action Plan

Instructions: Use this worksheet to create an action plan for understanding and sharing testimonies. Reflect on the biblical examples and your own experiences.

Biblical Examples of Testimonies:

- ☐ Choose one Old Testament and one New Testament example of testimonies.
- ☐ Write a brief reflection on each story and its impact on your faith.

Personal Testimony Moments:

- ☐ List key moments in your life when you've experienced God's grace.
- ☐ Select one moment to prepare for sharing as your testimony.

Sharing Testimony with a Friend:

- ☐ Identify a trusted friend with whom you'll share your testimony.

- Plan a conversation or meeting to share your testimony.

Overcoming Fears and Obstacles:

- Reflect on any fears or obstacles associated with sharing personal stories.
- Set specific goals to overcome these challenges.

In conclusion, testimonies are a vital part of faith and community. The Bible is filled with examples of individuals who shared their experiences with God, which, in turn, strengthened their faith and had a lasting impact on their communities. As you explore the importance of testimonies and practice sharing your own, you become a part of this rich tradition of faith and testimony. In the chapters that follow, we will continue to uncover the beauty of living a life of gratitude and sharing testimonies.

How to Share Your Testimony

Sharing your testimony is a powerful and deeply personal way to express your faith and inspire others. In this chapter, we will explore the process of crafting a personal testimony that is both genuine and impactful. We will offer guidance on how to effectively share your testimony in various settings, including church, community gatherings, and online platforms. Additionally, we will address common fears and obstacles associated with sharing personal stories, drawing from relevant Bible verses, providing explanations, offering details, and examples from both the Old and New Testaments. Finally, we will provide actionable plans to help you share your testimony confidently.

Crafting a Personal Testimony

A personal testimony is your unique story of faith, transformation, and encounters with God. It should be a genuine and heartfelt reflection of your journey. Consider these steps when crafting your testimony:

- ✓ **Begin with a Hook**: Start with an engaging introduction that captures your audience's attention. Share a moment of crisis, realization, or a significant event that prompted your faith journey.
- ✓ **Describe Your Journey**: Narrate your personal journey, including your life before encountering God, the circumstances that led you to seek faith, and how you encountered God's grace.
- ✓ **Express Your Transformation**: Explain how your life has changed as a result of your faith.

Share the impact of your relationship with God on your character, actions, and perspectives.

- ✓ **Highlight God's Role**: Emphasize how God has worked in your life. Describe the moments when you felt God's presence, guidance, or miraculous interventions.
- ✓ **End with a Resolution**: Conclude your testimony with a clear message of what you want your audience to take away. It could be an invitation to explore faith or a call to experience God's love.

Effective Sharing in Various Settings

- ✓ **In Church**: When sharing your testimony in a church setting, consider the audience's familiarity with faith. You can go deeper into spiritual aspects and use more biblical references.
- ✓ **Community Gatherings**: In a community setting, your testimony may reach a diverse audience. Keep it relatable and focus on universal themes of love, hope, and transformation.
- ✓ **Online Platforms**: Online platforms provide an opportunity to reach a global audience. Use social media, blogs, or podcasts to share your story. Visual aids like images or videos can enhance your message.

Addressing Common Fears and Obstacles

- ✓ **Fear of Judgment**: Understand that sharing your testimony is a deeply personal choice. While some may not resonate with your story, others will. Focus on the positive impact your testimony may have on someone's life.

- ✓ **Vulnerability**: Sharing your innermost thoughts and feelings can be intimidating. Remember that vulnerability can be a source of strength, allowing others to connect with your humanity.
- ✓ **Lack of Confidence**: It's natural to feel nervous. Practice sharing your testimony with a trusted friend or mentor first. Preparation and practice can boost your confidence.

Relevant Bible Verses and Examples

- ✓ **1 Peter 3:15-16**: "Always be prepared to give an answer to everyone who asks you to give the reason for the hope that you have. But do this with gentleness and respect." This verse encourages us to share our faith with humility and respect.
- ✓ **Acts 26:12-23**: In this passage, the Apostle Paul shares his testimony before King Agrippa, recounting his encounter with Christ on the road to Damascus. Paul's testimony is a powerful example of personal transformation and the impact it can have on others.

Action Plans for Sharing Your Testimony

- ✓ **Write It Down**: Start by writing a draft of your testimony, following the steps mentioned earlier.
- ✓ **Practice with a Friend**: Share your testimony with a trusted friend or mentor and ask for feedback.
- ✓ **Prepare for Questions**: Anticipate questions or concerns your audience might have and be prepared to address them.

- ✓ **Choose the Right Venue**: Select the most suitable platform or setting for sharing your testimony, taking into account your comfort level and your audience's receptiveness.
- ✓ **Pray for Guidance**: Seek divine guidance and pray for courage and clarity as you share your story.

Journaling Prompts:

- ✓ What elements would you include in your own personal testimony to make it genuine and impactful?
- ✓ Do you have any fears or concerns about sharing your testimony? How can you overcome them?
- ✓ Reflect on your experiences in different settings (church, community, online). In which setting do you feel most comfortable sharing your testimony?

Reflection Exercises:

- ✓ Practice sharing your testimony with a trusted friend or mentor and ask for feedback on your delivery and message.
- ✓ Attend a public speaking or storytelling workshop to improve your testimony-sharing skills.
- ✓ Prepare a short version of your testimony (elevator pitch) that you can use in casual conversations or when time is limited.

Action Plan

Instructions: Use this worksheet to create an action plan for effectively sharing your testimony. Set goals and actions for impactful sharing.

Crafting Your Testimony:

- Draft the key elements of your testimony, including your journey, challenges, and transformation.
- Edit and refine your testimony to make it genuine and impactful.

Sharing in Various Settings:

- List the different settings where you can share your testimony (e.g., church, community gatherings, online platforms).
- Research tips and strategies for effective testimony sharing in each setting.

Overcoming Fears and Obstacles:

- Identify common fears and obstacles related to sharing personal stories.
- Develop a plan to address and overcome these challenges.

Elevator Pitch Testimony:

- Create a concise version of your testimony (elevator pitch) for brief interactions.
- Practice delivering your elevator pitch to make it impactful.

Sharing your testimony is a profound act of faith and an opportunity to touch the lives of others. By crafting a genuine and impactful testimony and addressing common fears, you can inspire, uplift, and encourage those who hear your story. In the chapters that follow, we will continue to explore the beauty of gratitude, faith, and testimony in our spiritual journey.

Examples of Gratitude in the Bible

The Bible is rich with stories of gratitude and thanksgiving, both in the Old and New Testaments. In this chapter, we will explore these biblical examples in depth, examining the ways in which gratitude played a central role in the lives of various biblical figures. We will analyze how these figures expressed their gratitude and the consequences it had. Throughout, we will provide relevant Bible verses, detailed explanations, and examples from both the Old and New Testaments, as well as offer actionable plans to help you practice gratitude.

Old Testament Stories of Gratitude and Thanksgiving

- ✓ **Hannah's Song of Praise (1 Samuel 2:1-10)**: Hannah, who had longed for a child, praised God for giving her a son, Samuel. Her heartfelt gratitude is expressed in a beautiful song, highlighting God's sovereignty and her profound thankfulness.
- ✓ **King David's Thanksgiving (1 Chronicles 16:8-36)**: King David's psalms are filled with expressions of gratitude and thanksgiving. In this passage, he arranged for the Ark of the Covenant to be brought to Jerusalem and offered a psalm of thanksgiving to the Lord.
- ✓ **The Psalms of Thanksgiving**: The Book of Psalms is replete with songs of gratitude and thanksgiving. Psalms 100 and 136, in particular, are dedicated to praising God for His enduring love and faithfulness.

New Testament Passages of Gratitude

- ✓ **The Healing of the Ten Lepers (Luke 17:11-19)**: In this passage, Jesus heals ten lepers, but only one, a Samaritan, returns to express gratitude. Jesus commends the one who returned and tells him that his faith had made him well. This story highlights the importance of gratitude in faith.
- ✓ **The Feeding of the Five Thousand (Matthew 14:13-21)**: In this miracle, Jesus multiplies loaves and fish to feed the multitude. Before distributing the food, He gives thanks to God. This act of gratitude precedes a miraculous provision, demonstrating the power of thanksgiving.

Expressing Gratitude in the Bible

- ✓ **Sacrifices and Offerings**: In the Old Testament, expressions of gratitude often took the form of sacrifices and offerings at the temple. People would offer thanksgiving offerings to God.
- ✓ **Prayer and Praise**: Throughout the Bible, individuals expressed their gratitude through prayer and praise. The Psalms are a prime example, as they are filled with songs of gratitude and adoration.
- ✓ **Testimonies and Witness**: Sharing testimonies of God's goodness and grace was a common way to express gratitude and inspire others in the biblical narrative.

Consequences of Gratitude in the Bible

- ✓ **Spiritual Growth**: Expressing gratitude in the Bible is closely tied to spiritual growth. Those who showed gratitude often experienced a deepening of their faith and a closer relationship with God.

- ✓ **Community Building**: Gratitude also played a role in community building. Shared thanksgiving and celebrations brought people together, fostering unity and a sense of belonging.
- ✓ **Miraculous Intervention**: In some instances, expressing gratitude preceded or accompanied miraculous interventions and blessings, underscoring the significance of thanksgiving.

Action Plans for Practicing Gratitude

- ✓ **Daily Gratitude Practice**: Begin each day with a moment of gratitude, either through prayer or journaling, where you express thanks for the blessings in your life.
- ✓ **Share Your Thankfulness**: Let others know when you appreciate their actions or support. Gratitude is not only for God but for those around you.
- ✓ **Use the Psalms**: Read and reflect on the Psalms of thanksgiving in the Bible as a source of inspiration for your own prayers and expressions of gratitude.
- ✓ **Volunteer and Serve**: Get involved in charitable activities and volunteer work to express your gratitude for what you have by giving to others.

Journaling Prompts:

- ✓ What Old Testament story of gratitude resonates with you the most, and why?

- ✓ Which New Testament passage on gratitude do you find most inspiring, and how has it influenced your own perspective?
- ✓ How can you incorporate the principles of gratitude from the Bible into your daily life?

Reflection Exercises:

- ✓ Create a gratitude-themed art project or visual representation of your favorite biblical stories of gratitude.
- ✓ Join a group Bible study focused on gratitude and discuss the examples from both the Old and New Testaments.
- ✓ Share your favorite biblical story of gratitude with a friend or family member and discuss its relevance to your life.

In conclusion, the Bible provides a wealth of examples of gratitude and thanksgiving, demonstrating their significance in the lives of biblical figures. These stories serve as powerful reminders of the enduring importance of gratitude in our faith and daily lives. By studying and practicing gratitude in the ways shown by these biblical examples, you can deepen your relationship with God and foster a sense of community and unity with those around you. In the chapters that follow, we will continue to explore the transformative power of gratitude and faith.

Jesus as an Example of Gratitude

In this chapter, we will explore the life of Jesus as a profound example of gratitude. We will discuss instances in the Gospels where Jesus exhibited thankfulness, highlighting His teachings on gratitude and thankfulness. Additionally, we will reflect on the lessons that modern readers can draw from Jesus' example, supported by relevant Bible verses, explanations, and details from both the Old and New Testaments. We will also provide actionable plans for readers to practice gratitude inspired by Jesus' teachings.

Instances in the Gospels where Jesus Exhibited Gratitude

- ✓ **The Feeding of the Five Thousand (Matthew 14:13-21)**: Before multiplying the loaves and fish to feed the multitude, Jesus gave thanks. His act of gratitude preceded the miraculous provision of food, showing the power of thanksgiving.
- ✓ **The Raising of Lazarus (John 11:41-42)**: When Jesus arrived at the tomb of Lazarus, He gave thanks to God for hearing Him. He acknowledged God's presence and power before performing a miracle.
- ✓ **The Last Supper (Luke 22:17-20)**: During the Last Supper, Jesus took the bread and wine, gave thanks, and shared it with His disciples. This act of thanksgiving continues to be part of the Christian tradition in the form of Communion.

Jesus' Teachings on Thankfulness and Gratitude

- ✓ **The Parable of the Ten Lepers (Luke 17:11-19)**: Jesus healed ten lepers, but only one, a Samaritan, returned to express gratitude. He asked, "Where are the other nine?" and commended the one who returned. This parable emphasizes the importance of gratitude and thankfulness.
- ✓ **The Lord's Prayer (Matthew 6:9-13)**: In the Lord's Prayer, Jesus taught His disciples to begin their prayers by acknowledging God as "Our Father" and to pray for God's will to be done. This reflects a posture of submission and gratitude for God's guidance and provision.
- ✓ **Teachings on Generosity (Luke 6:38)**: Jesus encouraged generosity and taught that, "Give, and it will be given to you. A good measure, pressed down, shaken together and running over, will be poured into your lap. For with the measure you use, it will be measured to you." This teaching encourages a heart of gratitude in giving.

Lessons for Today from Jesus' Example

- ✓ **Gratitude as a Lifestyle**: Jesus' life exemplifies gratitude as a way of life, not just an occasional expression. Modern readers can learn to cultivate a consistent attitude of thankfulness.
- ✓ **Acknowledging God's Role**: Jesus consistently acknowledged God's role in His actions and miracles. Modern readers can recognize that gratitude involves acknowledging the divine source of blessings.

- ✓ **Prayerful Gratitude**: Jesus taught the importance of prayerful gratitude. Modern readers can incorporate thanksgiving into their daily prayers and express appreciation for the blessings they receive.
- ✓ **Generosity and Giving**: Jesus emphasized the principles of generosity and giving, demonstrating that gratitude extends beyond words to actions. Modern readers can apply these principles by giving to others and helping those in need.

Action Plans for Practicing Gratitude Inspired by Jesus

- ✓ **Daily Thankfulness Prayer**: Begin or end each day with a prayer of thanksgiving, expressing gratitude for the blessings in your life.
- ✓ **Generous Giving**: Practice generosity by giving to charitable causes or volunteering your time to help those in need.
- ✓ **Practice Acts of Kindness**: Make a conscious effort to perform acts of kindness for others, whether friends, family, or strangers.
- ✓ **Mindful Living**: Embrace mindfulness as a way to become more aware of the present moment and the many reasons to be thankful.
- ✓ **Regular Scripture Study**: Delve into the Gospels and other parts of the Bible to study Jesus' teachings on gratitude and consider how you can apply them in your life.

Journaling Prompts:

- ✓ Reflect on the instances where Jesus exhibited gratitude in the Gospels. How do His actions inspire you?
- ✓ How can you apply Jesus' teachings on thankfulness and gratitude in your own life?
- ✓ What lessons have you drawn from Jesus' example of gratitude?

Reflection Exercises:

- ✓ Spend time in prayer and meditation, focusing on the gratitude and humility of Jesus' actions as described in the Gospels.
- ✓ Create a visual representation of Jesus' acts of gratitude and use it as a reminder in your daily life.
- ✓ Engage in a group discussion or Bible study on the topic of Jesus as an example of gratitude and share your insights with others.

In conclusion, Jesus' life and teachings provide a profound example of gratitude and thankfulness. His actions and words emphasize the importance of acknowledging God's role, prayerful gratitude, generosity, and a lifestyle of thankfulness. By studying and practicing gratitude inspired by Jesus, modern readers can draw closer to God and live a life that reflects His teachings and example. In the chapters that follow, we will continue to explore the transformative power of gratitude and faith.

Testimonies from Real People

In this chapter, we will delve into real-life testimonies of individuals who have experienced God's grace and have chosen to share their stories. These testimonies will showcase the diversity of experiences and the common thread of gratitude that runs through them. We will demonstrate how these testimonies have profoundly impacted the lives of the individuals who shared them and those who heard them. Throughout, we will provide relevant Bible verses, explanations, details, and examples from both the Old and New Testaments. We will also offer actionable plans for readers to put into practice, inspired by the real-life experiences of these individuals.

Real-Life Testimonies of Grace and Gratitude

- ✓ **Grace's Healing Touch**: Grace, a young woman diagnosed with a life-threatening illness, shared her testimony of how God's healing touch led to her recovery. She expressed profound gratitude for the support of her community and the power of prayer, mirroring the story of the woman with the issue of blood (Mark 5:25-34) who experienced healing through her faith.
- ✓ **Recovery and Redemption**: Mark, a man who had struggled with addiction for years, shared his testimony of redemption and recovery. He attributed his transformation to his newfound faith in Christ, paralleling the story of the prodigal son (Luke 15:11-32) who experienced forgiveness and grace.

- ✓ **A Life Transformed**: Sarah, a single mother facing numerous challenges, shared her testimony of how her life had been transformed by faith. Her story echoed the experience of the Samaritan woman at the well (John 4:1-42), who encountered Jesus and, as a result, inspired her community.

Common Threads of Gratitude

- ✓ **Acknowledgment of God's Role**: In each testimony, there is a deep acknowledgment of God's role in the transformation of their lives. The individuals recognized that their experiences were not merely coincidences but manifestations of divine grace.
- ✓ **Community Support**: Gratitude is often directed not only towards God but also towards the support and love of their faith communities. The individuals' stories illustrate the importance of a supportive community in their journeys.
- ✓ **Acts of Service**: Many of these individuals expressed their gratitude by giving back and helping others who faced similar struggles. Their stories mirror the biblical principle of helping others with the comfort they themselves have received (2 Corinthians 1:3-4).

Impact of Testimonies

- ✓ **Inspiration and Hope**: These testimonies inspire and offer hope to those facing similar challenges. They serve as a reminder that transformation and healing are possible.

- ✓ **Strengthened Faith**: Sharing their stories strengthened the faith of the individuals who gave the testimonies. Their faith deepened as they saw the impact their stories had on others.
- ✓ **Community Bond**: Testimonies foster a sense of community and belonging. They create connections among individuals who share a common faith and inspire a culture of gratitude within the community.

Action Plans Inspired by Real-Life Testimonies

- ✓ **Share Your Story**: Reflect on your own life and the moments where you've experienced God's grace. Consider sharing your testimony within your faith community or online.
- ✓ **Active Listening**: Be an active listener when others share their testimonies. Offer support and encouragement, just as you would hope to receive.
- ✓ **Service and Giving**: Get involved in acts of service within your community or through charitable organizations. Make giving back a part of your gratitude practice.
- ✓ **Community Engagement**: Engage with your faith community, and participate in discussions and events that focus on sharing testimonies and gratitude.

Journaling Prompts:

- ✓ Reflect on the real-life testimonies shared in the book. Which one resonates with you the most, and why?

- ✓ Have you personally experienced a transformation that you would like to share as a testimony?
- ✓ How have these real-life testimonies reinforced the importance of gratitude and sharing one's experiences?

Reflection Exercises:

- ✓ Write a letter to one of the individuals who shared their real-life testimony in the book, expressing your appreciation for their story and the impact it had on you.
- ✓ Organize a small group gathering where each member shares a personal testimony of God's grace and transformation.
- ✓ Use the real-life testimonies as inspiration to develop your own testimony-sharing event within your community.

In conclusion, real-life testimonies are powerful reminders of the transformative power of God's grace and the role of gratitude in our faith journeys. By studying and learning from these testimonies, we can draw inspiration, deepen our faith, and foster a sense of community and hope among fellow believers. In the chapters that follow, we will continue to explore the beauty of gratitude, faith, and sharing testimonies in our spiritual journey.

Examples from Old and New Testament and How These Apply to us Today

Here are seven examples of characters from the Old Testament and seven from the New Testament who demonstrated gratitude and thanksgiving, along with how each of these examples can apply to us today:

Old Testament:

- ✓ **King David (Psalm 103):** King David was known for his heart of gratitude, as seen in Psalm 103, where he praised God for His mercy, forgiveness, and blessings. Today, we can learn from David to count our blessings, seek God's forgiveness, and express gratitude for His lovingkindness.
- ✓ **Hannah (1 Samuel 1):** Hannah's story of infertility and her heartfelt prayer of thanksgiving after giving birth to Samuel teaches us the power of persistent prayer and offering thanks for answered prayers.
- ✓ **Joseph (Genesis 45):** Joseph's forgiveness and gratitude toward his brothers, who had betrayed him, exemplify the healing power of gratitude in reconciling relationships. We can apply this lesson in forgiving and reconciling with others in our lives.
- ✓ **Job (Job 1:21):** Despite facing immense suffering, Job acknowledged God's sovereignty and maintained his gratitude. Job's story reminds us to maintain gratitude

even in difficult times, acknowledging God's authority over our lives.

- ✓ **Daniel (Daniel 6):** Daniel's unwavering faith and gratitude, even in the face of persecution, demonstrate the strength of a thankful heart. In today's world, we can draw inspiration from Daniel's example in standing firm in our faith and expressing gratitude amidst challenges.
- ✓ **The Israelites' Grumbling and Thanksgiving (Exodus 16):** The Israelites grumbled about their circumstances in the wilderness but learned to be thankful for manna from heaven. This teaches us to transition from complaining to gratitude in our own journeys.
- ✓ **The Psalmist (Psalm 136):** The author of Psalm 136 repeatedly emphasizes God's enduring love and thanksgiving for His mighty deeds. We can adopt this practice of giving thanks for God's unfailing love in our daily lives.

New Testament:

- ✓ **The Leper Who Returned (Luke 17:11-19):** The one leper who returned to thank Jesus demonstrates the importance of gratitude. We should apply this lesson by expressing thanks for the blessings we receive.
- ✓ **Mary, the Mother of Jesus (Luke 1:46-55):** Mary's Magnificat is a beautiful expression of gratitude and humility. We can apply her example by magnifying the Lord and acknowledging His greatness in our lives.
- ✓ **Zacchaeus (Luke 19:1-10):** Zacchaeus, after encountering Jesus, repented and expressed

his gratitude by giving back to those he had wronged. We can learn from him to express gratitude through acts of kindness and restitution.

- ✓ **The Woman With the Alabaster Jar (Matthew 26:6-13):** This woman's extravagant act of pouring perfume on Jesus' feet and wiping them with her hair is a profound expression of gratitude. We can emulate her by offering our best to God as an act of thanksgiving.
- ✓ **Paul (Philippians 4:4-7):** In his letter to the Philippians, Paul encourages rejoicing and thanksgiving in all circumstances. We can apply this by maintaining joy and gratitude, even in challenging situations.
- ✓ **The Prodigal Son (Luke 15:11-32):** The Prodigal Son's return and his father's gratitude teach us about God's forgiveness and unconditional love. We can apply this by seeking forgiveness and being grateful for God's grace.
- ✓ **The Apostle John (1 John 4:19):** John's words, "We love because he first loved us," emphasize the importance of gratitude for God's love. We should apply this by loving others in response to God's love and showing gratitude through love.

These examples from both the Old and New Testaments provide valuable insights into gratitude and thanksgiving, showing us how we can cultivate and express gratitude in various circumstances, making it relevant to our lives today.

Cultivating Gratitude: Overcoming Ingratitude and Embracing Blessings

The story of the ten lepers in the Bible, where only one returns to thank Jesus, serves as a poignant example of the challenge of cultivating gratitude. This situation raises important questions about why people often find it difficult to be grateful and how this attitude can be changed. Let's explore this issue in detail, along with practical steps, examples, and relevant Bible references.

Why People Find It Difficult to Be Grateful:

- ✓ **Entitlement Culture**: In today's society, many people have come to expect and feel entitled to certain comforts and blessings, making it harder to appreciate them.
- ✓ **Bible Reference**: In the Parable of the Prodigal Son (Luke 15:11-32), the older brother's sense of entitlement hindered his ability to celebrate his younger brother's return.
- ✓ **Comparison and Envy**: Comparing one's life to others can lead to envy and diminish the ability to be grateful for what one has.
- ✓ **Bible Reference**: The parable of the laborers in the vineyard (Matthew 20:1-16) illustrates the destructive nature of comparing one's blessings with others'.
- ✓ **Lack of Awareness**: People often fail to notice and appreciate the many daily

blessings they receive, taking them for granted.

- ✓ **Bible Reference**: The story of the feeding of the five thousand (Matthew 14:13-21) shows how the disciples initially failed to recognize the significance of the available food until Jesus blessed it.
- ✓ **Consumerism and Materialism**: A focus on material possessions and consumerism can lead to a constant desire for more, overshadowing gratitude.
- ✓ **Bible Reference**: In the story of the rich young ruler (Mark 10:17-31), the young man's attachment to his possessions hindered his gratitude for spiritual blessings.

How to Change This Attitude:

- ✓ Cultivate Mindfulness: Develop the habit of being mindful of the present moment and the blessings within it. Consider keeping a gratitude journal to record daily moments of thankfulness.
  Bible Reference: Psalm 118:24 - "This is the day that the Lord has made; let us rejoice and be glad in it."
  Example: Each morning, take a moment to appreciate the simple things in life, like the warmth of the sun or the taste of your morning coffee.
- ✓ Practice Generosity: Engage in acts of kindness and generosity towards others. Giving to those in need can help you recognize the abundance in your own life.
  Bible Reference: Luke 6:38 - "Give, and it will be given to you. A good measure, pressed

down, shaken together and running over, will be poured into your lap."
Example: Volunteer at a local charity or donate to a cause that resonates with you.

- ✓ Count Your Blessings: Take time to reflect on the blessings you have received. Consider creating a list of things you're thankful for and revisit it regularly.
  Bible Reference: Psalm 103:2 - "Bless the Lord, O my soul, and forget not all his benefits."
  Example: Make it a weekly ritual to reflect on the blessings that have come your way.
- ✓ Limit Social Comparison: Be mindful of how you engage with social media and how it influences your perception of others' lives. Unfollow accounts that trigger negative feelings of comparison and envy.
  Bible Reference: Galatians 6:4 - "Each one should test their own actions. Then they can take pride in themselves alone, without comparing themselves to someone else."
  Example: Consider taking regular breaks from social media to reset your perspective.
- ✓ Give Thanks in Prayer: Include thanksgiving in your daily prayers. Express gratitude for the blessings you've received and acknowledge the source of those blessings.
  Bible Reference: 1 Thessalonians 5:18 - "Give thanks in all circumstances; for this is the will of God in Christ Jesus for you."
  Example: Begin your prayers with expressions of gratitude before making requests.
- ✓ Learn from Past Mistakes: Reflect on moments when you failed to express gratitude

and consider how it affected your relationships and personal well-being. Use these experiences as opportunities for growth.
Bible Reference: Proverbs 27:6 - "Faithful are the wounds of a friend; profuse are the kisses of an enemy."
Example: Apologize to someone if your lack of gratitude has hurt them and strive to do better in the future.

- ✓ Celebrate the Blessings of Others: Rejoice in the successes and blessings of others, rather than feeling envious. Celebrating with others can foster gratitude and strengthen relationships.
Bible Reference: Romans 12:15 - "Rejoice with those who rejoice; weep with those who weep."
Example: Send a congratulatory message to a friend who has achieved a goal, and genuinely share in their joy.

Journaling Prompts:

- ✓ Reflect on a recent moment when you felt ungrateful or took something for granted. What triggered this feeling, and how did it affect your outlook?
- ✓ Think about a time when you received an unexpected blessing or act of kindness. Describe your feelings of gratitude and how it impacted your day.
- ✓ Consider the story of the ten lepers in the Bible (Luke 17:11-19). Put yourself in their shoes. Which leper do you relate to the most? Why?

- ✓ List five things you are grateful for in your life right now. Write down specific details about each one and how they make you feel.
- ✓ Explore the concept of scarcity mindset. Have there been times when you felt like there wasn't enough, and how did it affect your gratitude? How can you shift to an abundance mindset?

Reflection Exercises:

- ✓ Create a gratitude journal and commit to writing down three things you're thankful for each day. Review your entries at the end of the week and notice any patterns in your sources of gratitude.
- ✓ Consider making a list of people you appreciate in your life. Take the time to write a heartfelt note of thanks to one person on the list, expressing your gratitude for their presence.
- ✓ Reflect on the story of the ten lepers in Luke 17:11-19. What lessons can you draw from this story about gratitude, the power of thankfulness, and the significance of returning to give thanks?
- ✓ Practice mindfulness by engaging in a gratitude meditation. Close your eyes, take deep breaths, and visualize moments in your life that fill you with gratitude. How does this practice make you feel?
- ✓ Take a gratitude walk in nature. As you walk, focus on the beauty around you and reflect on the abundance of the world. How does this experience affect your sense of gratitude?
- ✓ Identify one area in your life where you struggle with ingratitude. Explore the root

causes of this ingratitude and brainstorm strategies to overcome it.

- ✓ Create a "Blessings Board" or a gratitude collage with images, words, or phrases that represent the things you're thankful for. Display it in a place where you can see it daily.
- ✓ Practice random acts of kindness and note the positive impact they have on both you and others. Reflect on how spreading kindness can enhance your gratitude.

Changing an attitude of ingratitude requires conscious effort, but it is a transformative journey. By cultivating mindfulness, practicing generosity, and learning from both biblical teachings and personal experiences, individuals can develop a heart of gratitude that enhances their relationships, mental well-being, and spiritual growth.

Encouraging a Culture of Gratitude

In this chapter, we will explore the importance of fostering a culture of gratitude within families, communities, and churches. We will provide practical suggestions for promoting thankfulness in various settings, and we'll encourage readers to take a proactive role in nurturing gratitude in their own lives and surroundings. Throughout, we will incorporate relevant Bible verses, explanations, details, and examples from both the Old and New Testaments. We will also offer actionable plans for readers to put into practice, inspired by the idea of fostering a culture of gratitude.

The Importance of Fostering a Culture of Gratitude

- ✓ **Strengthening Relationships**: A culture of gratitude promotes healthy, positive relationships within families, communities, and churches. Expressing thanks fosters understanding and unity among individuals.
- ✓ **Spiritual Growth**: Encouraging gratitude deepens spiritual growth by recognizing the source of blessings and acknowledging God's role in our lives.
- ✓ **Emotional Well-being**: Gratitude has a positive impact on emotional well-being. A culture of thankfulness reduces stress and enhances mental and emotional health.

Practical Suggestions for Promoting Thankfulness

- ✓ **Family Gratitude Rituals**: Create daily or weekly family rituals where everyone shares something they are thankful for. Encourage open and sincere expressions of gratitude.
- ✓ **Community Thanksgiving Events**: Organize community events that focus on thanksgiving and gratitude, such as potlucks or gatherings where people share their testimonies of God's goodness.
- ✓ **Thankful Church Services**: In churches, incorporate thanksgiving into services through songs, prayers, and testimonies. Dedicate time to reflect on the blessings of the congregation.
- ✓ **Gratitude Challenges**: Organize gratitude challenges within your community, encouraging members to share their thankfulness on social media or other platforms.

Biblical Inspiration and Examples

- ✓ **Colossians 3:15-17**: This passage emphasizes the importance of gratitude in our hearts, teaching and admonishing one another, and giving thanks in all circumstances. It underscores the role of thankfulness in the Christian community.
- ✓ **Psalm 100**: A Psalm of thanksgiving, this passage encourages us to make a joyful noise to the Lord, serve Him with gladness, and come into His presence with thanksgiving. It sets an example of communal praise and gratitude.

Action Plans to Foster a Culture of Gratitude

- ✓ **Model Gratitude**: Begin by setting an example of gratitude in your own life. Show appreciation for the people and blessings in your life.
- ✓ **Teach Thankfulness**: Teach the importance of gratitude to your children, family members, and community. Explain how expressing thanks benefits individuals and relationships.
- ✓ **Thankful Journal**: Start a gratitude journal where you jot down things you are thankful for each day. Encourage others to do the same.
- ✓ **Random Acts of Kindness**: Promote random acts of kindness within your community. Encourage people to perform small acts of generosity to express their gratitude.
- ✓ **Community Events**: Organize events that celebrate thanksgiving, where members share their stories of gratitude and blessings.

Journaling Prompts:

- ✓ How can you foster a culture of gratitude within your family, community, or church?
- ✓ Reflect on the practical suggestions provided in the chapter. Which ones resonate with you, and how can you implement them in your surroundings?
- ✓ Why is it important to actively participate in nurturing gratitude within your own life and environment?

Reflection Exercises:

- ✓ Create a gratitude action plan for your family or community. Determine specific steps and timelines for implementing gratitude practices.

- ✓ Organize or participate in a community event that focuses on gratitude and thanksgiving. Reflect on the impact it has on your community's culture.
- ✓ Begin a gratitude challenge within your family or community, encouraging members to share their thankfulness regularly.

In conclusion, fostering a culture of gratitude is essential for building strong relationships, supporting spiritual growth, and promoting emotional well-being. By implementing practical suggestions and taking inspiration from biblical examples, you can actively contribute to nurturing a culture of gratitude within your family, community, and church. In the chapters that follow, we will continue to explore the transformative power of gratitude and faith in our spiritual journey.

Gratitude and Testimony Sharing Progress Tracker

Instructions: *Use this tracker to monitor your progress in cultivating gratitude and sharing testimonies. Each section corresponds to a chapter in the book, and you can mark your progress and reflections as you go along. You may want to revisit this tracker periodically to see how far you've come in your journey.*

Chapter 1: The Power of Gratitude

- ☐ Started a gratitude journal.
- ☐ Shared moments of gratitude with friends or family.
- ☐ Practiced gratitude meditation.
- ☐ Recognized the impact of gratitude on my life.

Chapter 2: Why Share Testimonies?

- ☐ Reflected on personal experiences of God's grace.
- ☐ Identified the significance of sharing testimonies.
- ☐ Listened to testimonies that inspired me.
- ☐ Recognized the value of sharing my own testimony.

Chapter 3: Building a Grateful Heart

- ☐ Cultivated mindfulness in daily life.
- ☐ Engaged in acts of kindness and generosity.
- ☐ Maintained a gratitude journal.
- ☐ Replaced negative thoughts with gratitude.

Chapter 4: Importance of Testimonies

- ☐ Explored biblical examples of testimonies.
- ☐ Discussed the significance of sharing testimonies.
- ☐ Created a list of personal testimony moments.
- ☐ Shared my testimony with a trusted friend.

Chapter 5: How to Share Your Testimony

- ☐ Crafted a personal and impactful testimony.
- ☐ Practiced sharing my testimony with a friend or mentor.
- ☐ Attended a testimony-sharing event or church service.
- ☐ Overcame common fears or obstacles associated with sharing.

Chapter 6: Examples of Gratitude in the Bible

- ☐ Explored Old Testament stories of gratitude.
- ☐ Examined New Testament passages on gratitude.
- ☐ Analyzed how biblical figures expressed their gratitude.
- ☐ Shared a favorite biblical story of gratitude with others.

Chapter 7: Jesus as an Example of Gratitude

- ☐ ☐Discussed instances where Jesus exhibited gratitude.
- ☐ Highlighted Jesus' teachings on thankfulness.
- ☐ Reflected on the lessons drawn from Jesus' example.
- ☐ Applied Jesus' teachings to my own life.

Chapter 8: Testimonies from Real People

- ☐ Read real-life testimonies from the book.

- ☐ Identified with one or more of the featured individuals.
- ☐ Reflected on the impact of these testimonies.
- ☐ Prepared to share my own testimony.

Chapter 9: Encouraging a Culture of Gratitude

- ☐ Fostered a culture of gratitude within my family or community.
- ☐ Practiced practical suggestions for promoting thankfulness.
- ☐ Participated in community events focused on gratitude.
- ☐ Demonstrated proactive nurturing of gratitude.

Use symbols, such as a checkmark (√) or color coding, to mark your progress in each section. Revisit this progress tracker as you continue your journey, and celebrate your growth and transformation along the way.

Progress Key: √ = Started √√ = In Progress
√√√ = Completed [Date] = Date of Completion

This progress tracker provides a visual representation of your journey towards a more grateful and testimony-sharing life. By checking off completed activities, you can see your growth over time and feel a sense of accomplishment. It also encourages you to actively engage with the book's content and apply what you've learned.

31 Bible Verses with a Positive Decree and Declaration for Daily Reflection and Prophecy

Here is a list of 31 relevant Bible verses on gratitude and sharing testimonies. Each verse is accompanied by a positive decree and declaration that you can use for daily reflection and prophecy over your life. Use these daily verses and declarations to strengthen your faith, cultivate gratitude, and embrace the power of sharing testimonies with others.

Day 1: Psalm 107:1 *Verse: "Give thanks to the Lord, for he is good; his love endures forever."* **Declaration**: I declare that God's goodness and love are with me always. I will give thanks and praise to Him every day.

Day 2: Psalm 136:26 *Verse: "Give thanks to the God of heaven. His love endures forever."* **Declaration**: I declare that God's love endures forever, and I will give thanks to the God of heaven, who watches over me.

Day 3: 1 Thessalonians 5:18 *Verse: "Give thanks in all circumstances; for this is God's will for you in Christ Jesus."* **Declaration**: I declare that I will give thanks in all circumstances, knowing that it aligns with God's will for my life.

Day 4: Colossians 3:17 *Verse: "And whatever you do, whether in word or deed, do it all in the name of the Lord Jesus, giving thanks to God the Father through him."* **Declaration**: I declare that in everything I do, I will give thanks to God through Jesus Christ.

Day 5: Psalm 9:1 *Verse: "I will give thanks to you, Lord, with all my heart; I will tell of all your wonderful deeds."* **Declaration**: I declare that I will give thanks to the Lord with all my heart and share His wonderful deeds with others.

Day 6: Psalm 105:1 *Verse: "Give praise to the Lord, proclaim his name; make known among the nations what he has done."* **Declaration**: I declare that I will proclaim the name of the Lord and make known His deeds to all nations.

Day 7: Psalm 66:16 *Verse: "Come and hear, all you who fear God; let me tell you what he has done for me."* **Declaration**: I declare that I will share what God has done for me with all who seek Him.

Day 8: Psalm 78:4 *Verse: "We will not hide them from their descendants; we will tell the next generation the praiseworthy deeds of the Lord, his power, and the wonders he has done."* **Declaration**: I declare that I will share God's praiseworthy deeds and wonders with the next generation.

Day 9: Revelation 12:11 *Verse: "They triumphed over him by the blood of the Lamb and by the word of their testimony."* **Declaration**: I declare that I will triumph over challenges through the blood of the Lamb and the power of my testimony.

Day 10: Mark 5:19 *Verse: "Go home to your own people and tell them how much the Lord has done for you, and how he has had mercy on you."* **Declaration**: I declare that I will go and tell my own people about the mercy and grace the Lord has bestowed upon me.

Day 11: Psalm 34:2 *Verse: "I will glory in the Lord; let the afflicted hear and rejoice."* **Declaration**: I declare that I will glory in the Lord, and my testimony will bring joy to the afflicted.

Day 12: 2 Corinthians 9:11 *Verse: "You will be enriched in every way so that you can be generous on every occasion, and through us your generosity will result in thanksgiving to God."* **Declaration**: I declare that I will be enriched to be generous, and my generosity will bring thanksgiving to God.

Day 13: 2 Corinthians 1:3-4 *Verse: "Praise be to the God and Father of our Lord Jesus Christ, the Father of compassion and the God of all comfort, who comforts us in all our troubles, so that we can comfort those in any trouble with the comfort we ourselves receive from God."* **Declaration**: I declare that I will share the comfort I receive from God with others in their times of trouble.

Day 14: Psalm 40:10 *Verse: "I do not hide your righteousness in my heart; I speak of your faithfulness and your saving help. I do not conceal your love and your faithfulness from the great assembly."* **Declaration**: I declare that I will speak of God's faithfulness, love, and saving help openly to the assembly.

Day 15: Matthew 10:32 *Verse: "Whoever acknowledges me before others, I will also acknowledge before my Father in heaven."* **Declaration**: I declare that I will acknowledge and testify about Jesus before others, and He will acknowledge me before the Father in heaven.

Day 16: 2 Samuel 22:50 *Verse: "For this, I will praise you, Lord, among the nations; I will sing the praises of your name."* **Declaration**: I declare that I will praise the Lord among the nations and sing the praises of His name.

Day 17: Psalm 145:4 *Verse: "One generation commends your works to another; they tell of your mighty acts."* **Declaration**: I declare that I will commend God's works to the next generation and share His mighty acts.

Day 18: Isaiah 12:4 *Verse: "In that day you will say: 'Give thanks to the Lord, call on his name; make known among the nations what he has done, and proclaim that his name is exalted.'"* **Declaration**: I declare that I will call on the Lord's name and make known among the nations what He has done, proclaiming His exalted name.

Day 19: Psalm 92:1-2 *Verse: "It is good to praise the Lord and make music to your name, O Most High, proclaiming your love in the morning and your faithfulness at night."* **Declaration**: I declare that I will praise the Lord and proclaim His love and faithfulness in both the morning and the night.

Day 20: Psalm 118:17 *Verse: "I will not die but live, and will proclaim what the Lord has done."* **Declaration**: I declare that I will live and proclaim what the Lord has done for me.

Day 21: 1 Peter 3:15 *Verse: "But in your hearts revere Christ as Lord. Always be prepared to give an answer to everyone who asks you to give the reason for the hope that you have."* **Declaration**: I declare that I will revere Christ as Lord and be ready to share the reason for the hope within me.

Day 22: Luke 12:8 *Verse: "I tell you, whoever publicly acknowledges me before others, the Son of Man will also acknowledge before the angels of God."* **Declaration**: I declare that I will publicly acknowledge Jesus before others, and He will acknowledge me before the angels of God.

Day 23: Psalm 30:12 *Verse: "that my heart may sing your praises and not be silent. Lord my God, I will praise you forever."* **Declaration**: I declare that my heart will sing praises to the Lord, and I will praise Him forever.

Day 24: Romans 1:16 *Verse: "For I am not ashamed of the gospel because it is the power of God that brings salvation to everyone who believes."* **Declaration**: I declare that I am not ashamed of the gospel, for it is the power of God for salvation.

Day 25: 1 Chronicles 16:8 *Verse: "Give praise to the Lord, proclaim his name; make known among the nations what he has done."* **Declaration**: I declare that I will give praise to the Lord and make known among the nations what He has done.

Day 26: Psalm 107:2 *Verse: "Let the redeemed of the Lord tell their story—those he redeemed from the hand of the foe."* **Declaration**: I declare that I am one of the redeemed of the Lord, and I will tell my story of His redemption.

Day 27: Acts 1:8 *Verse: "But you will receive power when the Holy Spirit comes on you, and you will be my witnesses in Jerusalem, and in all Judea and Samaria, and to the ends of the earth."* **Declaration**: I declare that I have received power from the Holy Spirit, and I am Christ's witness to the ends of the earth.

Day 28: Psalm 145:3 *Verse: "Great is the Lord and most worthy of praise; his greatness no one can fathom."* **Declaration**: I declare that the Lord is great and most worthy of praise, and His greatness is beyond human comprehension.

Day 29: Romans 10:10 *Verse: "For it is with your heart that you believe and are justified, and it is with your mouth that you profess your faith and are* *saved."* **Declaration**: I declare that with my heart, I believe and am justified, and with my mouth, I profess my faith and am saved.

Day 30: Psalm 9:11 *Verse: "Sing the praises of the Lord, enthroned in Zion; proclaim among the nations what he has done."* **Declaration**: I declare that I will sing praises to the Lord, who is enthroned in Zion, and I will proclaim what He has done among the nations.

Day 31: Ephesians 5:20 *Verse: "always giving thanks to God the Father for everything, in the name of our Lord Jesus Christ."* **Declaration**: I declare that I will always give thanks to God the Father for everything in the name of our Lord Jesus Christ.

"THANKFULNESS"- the 12 Steps to Practice Gratitude Daily

This **"THANKFULNESS"** acronym outlines a comprehensive approach to practicing gratitude daily, helping you cultivate a thankful and appreciative mindset in various aspects of your life.

T - Take Notice: Begin your gratitude practice by taking notice of the things around you. Pay attention to the details and blessings in your life. Verse: "This is the day the Lord has made; let us rejoice and be glad in it." (Psalm 118:24)

H - Have a Gratitude Journal: Maintain a gratitude journal to record your daily blessings and moments of thankfulness. Write down what you're thankful for. Verse: "I will give thanks to you, Lord, with all my heart; I will tell of all your wonderful deeds." (Psalm 9:1)

A - Appreciate the Present: Focus on the present moment. Embrace the "now" and appreciate the beauty in your life at this very moment. Verse: "Therefore do not worry about tomorrow, for tomorrow will worry about itself. Each day has enough trouble of its own." (Matthew 6:34)

N - Nurture Relationships: Be grateful for the people in your life. Nurture your relationships and express your appreciation to those who matter most. Verse: "Two are better than one, because they have a good return for their labor." (Ecclesiastes 4:9)

K - Kind Acts of Giving: Engage in acts of kindness and giving. By helping others, you'll often find even more reasons to be grateful. Verse: "Give, and it will be given to you. A good measure, pressed down, shaken together and running over, will be poured into your lap. For with the measure you use, it will be measured to you." (Luke 6:38)

F - Find Joy in Small Things: Recognize the joy in the little things in life. It's often the small moments that bring the greatest happiness. Verse: "You make known to me the path of life; you will fill me with joy in your presence, with eternal pleasures at your right hand." (Psalm 16:11)

U - Understand Your Blessings: Take time to truly understand the blessings you have. Reflect on the significance and impact they hold in your life. Verse: "Every good and perfect gift is from above, coming down from the Father of the heavenly lights, who does not change like shifting shadows." (James 1:17)

L - Learn from Challenges: Gratitude doesn't mean ignoring challenges but learning from them. Be thankful for the lessons adversity brings. Verse: "Consider it pure joy, my brothers and sisters, whenever you face trials of many kinds, because you know that the testing of your faith produces perseverance." (James 1:2-3)

N - Notice Growth: Notice your personal growth and how gratitude positively influences your well-being. Acknowledge the changes and improvements in your life. Verse: "But the fruit of the Spirit is love, joy, peace, forbearance, kindness, goodness, faithfulness, gentleness and self-control. Against such things there is no law." (Galatians 5:22-23)

E - Embrace Positivity: Embrace a positive attitude. Let gratitude be the foundation for your overall outlook and approach to life. Verse: "Do not be anxious about anything, but in every situation, by prayer and petition, with thanksgiving, present your requests to God." (Philippians 4:6)

S - Share Your Gratitude: Share your gratitude with others. Express your thankfulness and inspire those around you to practice gratitude as well. Verse: "Let the message of Christ dwell among you richly as you teach and admonish one another with all wisdom through psalms, hymns, and songs from the Spirit, singing to God with gratitude in your hearts." (Colossians 3:16)

S - Stay Consistent: Make gratitude a consistent practice in your daily life. The more you practice, the more it becomes a natural part of who you are. Verse: "Rejoice always, pray continually, give thanks in all circumstances; for this is God's will for you in Christ Jesus." (1 Thessalonians 5:16-18)

Songs of Gratitude And Thanksgiving

Here are 2 Songs of Gratitude and Thanksgiving inspired by 2 Samuel 7:18-22. These songs are a heartfelt expression of thanks to God for His blessings and miraculous works in my life. Use your own melodies to sing them out loud to HIM

Verse 1:
In humble awe, I bow my head,
For all Your grace, my heart is fed.
My life, a testimony, Lord, it's true,
In thankfulness, I turn to You.

Chorus:
I lift my voice in gratitude and praise,
To You, O Lord, my song I raise.
You've brought me far, a miraculous life,
In Your embrace, I find no strife.

Verse 2:
Salvation's gift, my soul set free,
Your endless love, my family tree.
My children and my grandchildren dear,
A legacy of faith, so crystal clear.

Repeat Chorus

Verse 3:
In health and wealth, I'm richly blessed,
Your joy in every trial, I've confessed.
With prosperous heart and soul, I'll sing,
A testament to Your boundless wing.

Repeat Chorus

Verse 4:
When people see the love we share,
They'll know Your presence is everywhere.
May lives be touched, may hearts be swayed,
To glorify the God who never fades.

Repeat Chorus

Verse 5:
For those who thank with hearts full and true,
Find in Your blessings, love anew.
Thanksgiving's gateway to multiplication's store,
In gratitude, I'll praise You evermore.

Repeat Chorus

Verse 6:
So here's my song, from Gerard to God,
A heartfelt thanks for the path I've trod.
With thankful heart, I'll forever sing,
Of Your love, grace, and blessings, My King of Kings.

Repeat Chorus

Song 2

Chorus:
In gratitude, I lift my voice,
To You, my Lord, my heart's true choice.
For all You've done, I sing this praise,
In joyful thanks, my voice I raise.

Verse 1:
Oh, Lord, I stand in awe of You,
For all Your wondrous deeds so true.
Salvation's grace, a precious gift,
In Your embrace, my soul does lift.

Repeat Chorus

Verse 2:
My family, a cherished treasure,
With love that knows no bound or measure.
Children and grandchildren, blessings untold,
In their laughter, Your love unfolds.

Repeat Chorus

Verse 3:
In health and wealth, Your hand I see,
Prosperity and joy, bestowed on me.
Miraculous life, I can't deny,
Your grace, my God, lifts me so high.

Repeat Chorus

Verse 4:
When others see the life I live,
The testimony Your grace does give.

In thankfulness, Your name we glorify,
Multiplying blessings as we magnify.

Repeat Chorus

Verse 5:
I've found that thankfulness is the key,
To open doors and set hearts free.
Gratitude's the gateway to multiplication,
In Your love, we find our salvation.

Repeat Chorus

Verse 6:
So, Lord, I offer up this song,
A melody of praise, sweet and strong.
With gratitude, my heart overflows,
In thanksgiving, our love steadily grows.

Chorus:
In gratitude, I lift my voice,
To You, my Lord, my heart's true choice.
For all You've done, I sing this praise,
In joyful thanks, my voice I raise.

May these songs of gratitude and thanksgiving reflect the depth of your heart's devotion and your appreciation for God's blessings in your life.

Conclusion

In this concluding chapter, we will summarize the key points and takeaways from the book. We will encourage readers to embrace gratitude as a way of life and to share their testimonies with enthusiasm and humility. Additionally, we will offer a final inspirational message about the beauty of living with a grateful heart. Throughout, we will incorporate relevant Bible verses, explanations, details, and examples from both the Old and New Testaments. We will provide actionable plans for readers to put into practice, inspired by the teachings and stories shared in this book.

Key Points and Takeaways

- ✓ **Gratitude Transforms Lives**: We have explored how gratitude has the power to transform lives by fostering positive emotions, improving mental health, and deepening spiritual connections.
- ✓ **Sharing Testimonies Matters**: Sharing testimonies is an essential part of living a life of gratitude. We've seen how the act of sharing personal encounters with God can inspire others and strengthen our faith.
- ✓ **Biblical Inspiration**: Throughout the book, we've drawn inspiration from the Bible, witnessing the examples of gratitude and thanksgiving in both the Old and New Testaments. These stories serve as timeless reminders of the importance of gratitude.
- ✓ **Real-Life Testimonies**: Real people have shared their stories of transformation and

grace, illustrating the impact of gratitude and the importance of sharing testimonies.

Embrace Gratitude as a Way of Life

The journey of gratitude is not merely about understanding its significance; it's about embracing it as a way of life. As you close this book, I encourage you to take the following steps:

- ✓ **Daily Gratitude Practice**: Make gratitude a part of your daily routine. Begin or end each day by acknowledging the blessings in your life. A gratitude journal can be a valuable tool.
- ✓ **Share Your Testimony**: Reflect on your encounters with God, the moments of grace, and the times when gratitude has transformed your life. Share your testimonies with enthusiasm and humility.
- ✓ **Give Back**: As you experience the power of gratitude, give back to your community and those in need. Acts of kindness and service not only express your gratitude but also inspire it in others.
- ✓ **Practice Mindfulness**: Embrace mindfulness as a way to become more aware of the present moment and the many reasons to be thankful.

The Beauty of Living with a Grateful Heart

Living with a grateful heart is a beautiful journey filled with blessings and transformative experiences. When we embrace gratitude, we see the world through a different lens. We find hope in challenging times, strength in our faith, and purpose in our actions.

In Matthew 6:21, Jesus teaches us, "For where your treasure is, there your heart will be also." By making gratitude your treasure, you open your heart to a world filled with wonder and appreciation. When your heart is filled with gratitude, you not only recognize the goodness of God in your life but also become a beacon of light for others.

Journaling Prompts:

- ✓ What are your key takeaways from the book on gratitude and sharing testimonies?
- ✓ How can you implement the teachings and practices discussed in the book into your daily life?
- ✓ Reflect on the final inspirational message about living with a grateful heart. How can you make this a reality in your life?

Reflection Exercises:

- ✓ Write a letter to your future self, outlining your commitment to living with a grateful heart and how you plan to inspire others with your journey.
- ✓ Create a vision board that visually represents your aspirations for a life filled with gratitude and the impact you hope to make on others.
- ✓ Share your reflections and gratitude action plan with a close friend or family member and ask for their support and accountability in your journey.

As you continue your journey, remember that gratitude is not an isolated practice but a way of life that influences your actions, relationships, and spiritual growth. May your life be a testament to the power of gratitude, and may you inspire others to join you on this beautiful path.

In the chapters that have unfolded, we've explored the transformative power of gratitude, the importance of sharing testimonies, and the examples set by biblical figures and real people who have embraced gratitude. Let your journey be a reflection of these teachings, and let your life be a living testimony of the beauty of a grateful heart.

About the Author
'GERARD ASSEY'

Gerard Assey is a Graduate in Economics, a PGD in Management (HRD) and holds a Doctorate in Leadership. Gerard holds several International Qualifications in Sales, Debt Collection, Training & Teaching, and is a 'Fellow' of the prestigious 'Institute of Sales & Marketing Management'-UK, a Certified NLP Practitioner, a 'Certified Trainer', an 'Accredited Management Teacher-Behavioral Sciences', a 'Certified Competency Facilitator', a 'Certified Management Consultant'- (the International credentials of a professional management consultant, awarded in accordance with global standards of the ICMCI); and a Certification from the University of Michigan in 'Successful Negotiation: Essential Strategies and Skills'

He is also a Member of the 'National Association of Sales Professionals' backed with several years experience in varied industries, both in India and Overseas. He also holds an 'Etiquette Consultant' Certification from the USA (by Sue Fox, Author of Best Seller: 'Business Etiquette for Dummies'. She has trained some of the top celebrities' world over). He was also a recipient of a scholarship for extensive training in Japan on 'Corporate Management for India'.

Gerard Assey is 'Founder & Chief Corporate Trainer' of the Group: '**Citius, Altius, Fortius Unlimited**'- an organization that **celebrated 20 years of Glorious Service** in 2021, focusing on 3 Core Competencies:

People. Performance. Profit; in functional areas of Sales & Marketing, HR & Organizational Development, covering Recruitment, Training & Consultancy!

Having managed organizations with large Sales Forces in India & Overseas, his specialization cover extensive areas of Sales Training (All levels - Presentation, Negotiation, Key/ Strategic Accounts Management & Managerial Skills for all sectors), Bid Proposal/ Capture Planning/ Management Trainings, Retail Sales, Customer Service & Customer Retention Programs, Training for Prevention & Collection of Debt, Self & Personal Development Programs (Time Management, Teamwork & Team Building, Business Etiquette & Personal Grooming, Leadership & Managerial Skills, People Management Skills, Train-the-Trainer etc), including preparation of Custom-designed Business Manuals for Internal (HR, Induction, and Sales etc) & External use (Instruction, User Manuals).

Gerard has successfully conducted over 6000 Trainings & Workshops (as of Dec '23) all across India, Middle East, Africa, Europe & S.E. Asia. Besides public programs conducted regularly, both in India & Overseas, he has some of the top names as clients whom he services from Single Owners to large Public & Government undertakings, covering all sectors, for their in-house needs.

His website: www.CollectionSkills.com is the only one in this part of the world to be featured in the 'Collections & Credit Risk Magazine-USA' under 'Who's Who in Training' and ranks TOP, along with other websites listed below on most search engines.

Gerard is author of 99 books already (Dec 2023),

A few of our business related books:

1. Bite-sized Bits on Commonsense Management
2. Heart to Heart on Life's Principles'
3. How to become a Successful Manager
4. The Sales Professionals' Master Workbook of S.Y.S.T.E.M.S
5. The Professional Business Email Etiquette Handbook & Guide
6. The Professional Business Video-Conferencing Etiquette Handbook & Guide
7. Professional Presentation Skills
8. Exceptional Customer Service
9. Professional Tele-Marketing Skills
10. Professional Debt Collection Skills
11. The G.R.E.A.T. Sales & Service Workbook
12. Sales Training Advantage for Results (*The Ultimate Sales Training Manual to enable you stand out as a S.T.A.R.*)
13. CEO Daily Planner & Organizer
14. The Sales Professionals' Master Daily Planner
15. The Professional Debt Collector's Master Daily Planner
16. My Daily Planner & Organizer
17. MY EMERGENCY INFORMATION RECORD (Family Emergency & Peace of Mind Planner)
18. The Ultimate Therapist & Counselors Planner and Organizer
19. Building an Ethical Workplace
20. Managing Relationships at Work
21. Managing Business Meetings Effectively
22. Effective Delegation Skills
23. Goal Setting for Success
24. B2B Selling by Email
25. Professional Business Etiquette & Grooming
26. Dining Etiquette & Table Manners
27. Effective Networking Skills
28. Grooming, Etiquette & Manners for Teens, Young Adults & Future Leaders
29. Inter-Personal Skills
30. Get Ready, Get Hired!
31. Selling in a Recession
32. Effective Receivables Management in an Economic Downturn!
33. Real Estate & Property Sales Training
34. Credit Sales & Accounts Receivable Management
35. Selling Skills for Real Estate & Property Advisors
36. Take G.R.E.A.T. C.A.R.E!
37. Spa, Salon & Health Club Selling Skills
38. Selling Travel, Holiday & MICE Services
39. Selling Skills for Spa's, Salons & Health Clubs
40. Retailing in Salons & Spas

41. Selling Holiday, Vacation, Tours & Packages
42. The Power of Sales Referrals
43. Selling Luxury
44. Technical Selling Skills
45. Financial Advisors Sales Training
46. Dealing with Burnout at Work Monopolize Your Markets
47. Selling to Affluent Customers
48. Growing up with Grace
49. Financial Selling Skills
50. *The Effective Manager's Guide: Key Skills to Thrive*
51. From Aspiring to Inspiring: A Guide for New Managers on the Rise
52. The Power of Focus
53. Selling with Integrity: Sell Like Jesus The Perfect Role Model!
54. 31 Habits of Champions: Your 31-Day Journey to Greatness
55. Rejecting Grasshopper Talk: From Grasshopper to Giant-Killer-*Defeating Giants Daily!*
56. Navigate the AI-Powered Future of Bid & Proposals: Up-Skill to Stay Relevant with Alternative Career Paths & Opportunities
57. Hiring Sales Winners
58. Present with Impact
59. Success Unlocked: *Breaking Free from Habits that Hold You Back*
60. Complaints to Cheers, Feedback to Gold: Mastering Complaints Management
61. Thriving Together: *Cultivating Diversity, Equity, and Inclusion*
62. Coaching Skills for Sales Managers
63. Soaring to Success in Business & Leadership: Swifter, Higher, Stronger!
64. From Classroom to Podium: A Student's Guide to Powerful Public Speaking & Presentation Skills
65. Developing Self-Discipline
66. The CEO's 31-Day Power Plan: Unlocking Success through Essential Traits
67. Credibility Matters
68. A Winning Attitude
69. Bid & Proposal Management Using AI

From the Ministry side, Gerard graduated in the very first batch of Charis Bible College-India & had for over 9 years served as a Part-time Faculty at Charis Bible College-Chennai (Andrew Wommack Ministries-Colorado, USA).
He is also a graduate of the Advanced Mentorship Program (AMP) and the Circle Of Ministerial Engagement (C.O.M.E.) of Prophet Jerome Fernando and a Spiritual Son of the Esteemed Prophet.
An accomplished author of several Secular & Christian Books, Gerard has been on the board of a few international organizations and boasts of being the SON of the MOST HIGH GOD: An ordinary guy following an extraordinary GOD!

...And some of his most recent Christian Books being:

1. A Bouquet of Praises for My KING
2. Christian Jokes for the Serious Religious' Folks!
3. Jesus Healed You!
4. Praise24Ever! (also in Tamil version)
5. The 5G Network of GOD
6. Building Faith over F.E.A.R- FACE EVERYTHING AND RISE with JESUS
7. Hebrew and Greek Praise and Worship Words
8. Godly Mothers' and Grandmothers' Bible Story time for Kids!
9. Miracles of Jesus in Pictures
10. Raise your Praise all 365 Days
11. Thanking GOD with an Attitude of Gratitude
12. Meditating on the Attributes of GOD
13. Puppet Scripts
14. Alcohol Ruins, JESUS Reforms, Renews & Restores!
15. Habakkuk 2:2 Christian Daily Journal, Planner & Organizer
16. ABC of GOD's Word for Handwriting Practice
17. Daily Bible Verse Handwriting Practice (Building Godly Character & Faith through Cursive Handwriting Practice!)
18. Guiding Light: Fun & Faith-Building Bible Activities for Children
19. Rejecting Grasshopper Talk: From Grasshopper to Giant-Killer-*Defeating Giants Daily!*
20. Teen Titans of Faith: *Building Courage, Determination & Christ-like-Esteem*
21. I AM Empowered: *Unleashing Divine Power with Positive Declarations*
22. Be A Solution Provider-*From Passion to Purpose*: *A Biblical*

Guide to Being the Answer to the World!

23. Miracles of JESUS
24. Parables of Jesus for a Meaningful Life!
25. A Grateful Heart: Importance of Sharing Testimonies of GOD's Grace

Besides regularly contributing to business & trade journals, including international ones such as the 'Creative Training Techniques' and the 'Sales News' of the U.S.A, He is also a member of several prestigious bodies & trade associations, having participated in many Conferences & Workshops in India & Overseas.

Prior to his last assignment of leading & managing a large MNC as head, Gerard had a 3-year stint in the Middle East as a Consultant with a leading British Consultancy Firm.

As the past 'Official Country Representative' for the International Business Award- 'THE STEVIES'-(the business world's own Oscar) for about 4 years- he ensured a few Indian companies that qualify for the same every year!

Gerard can be contacted at:

Email: training@Sales-Training.in,training@CollectionSkills.com
Websites:

www.Sales-Training.in
www.EtiquetteWorks.in
www.CollectionSkills.com
www.RetailSalesTraining.in
www.SalesTrainingIndia.com
www.ManualPreparation.com
www.TrainingWithPuppets.com
www.FirstContactAcademy.com
www.SalesAndMarketingRecruiter.com

Our TRAININGS that can help your team

- ✓ **Sales Effectiveness**: Selling Skills for any Sector: Service/ Logistics/ FMCG Realty/ Insurance & Finance/ Media/ SPA's, Health Clubs & Salons/ Key Account Management, Effective Negotiation Skills/ Bid & Proposal Management Skills/ Retail Sales Training: Any Sector (Auto, Jewelry, Clothing, Luxury etc)
- ✓ **Customer Service Skills**-Complaints Handling & Customer Retention
- ✓ **Debt Prevention & Collection Skills**
- ✓ **Etiquette & Grooming**
- ✓ **Leadership & Managerial Skills**
- ✓ **Self & Personal Development Skills**: Presentation Skills/ Effective Communication Skills/Business Proposal Writing Skills/ Problem Solving & Decision Making Skills/ Empowering Secretaries-The perfect PA! (For Secretaries & PA's)/ Effective Time Management/ Teamwork & Teambuilding/ P.R.I.D.E- **P**ersonal **R**esponsibility **I**n **D**elivering **E**xcellence

www.ingramcontent.com/pod-product-compliance
Lightning Source LLC
LaVergne TN
LVHW010118170826
845678LV00012B/2471

9788196720292